SWEET VICTORY

Lance Armstrong's
Incredible Journey

THE AMAZING STORY OF THE GREATEST COMEBACK IN SPORTS

BY
MARK STEWART

THE MILLBROOK PRESS
BROOKFIELD, CONNECTICUT

M

THE MILLBROOK PRESS

Produced by
BITTERSWEET PUBLISHING
John Sammis, President
and
TEAM STEWART, INC.

Series Design and Electronic Page Makeup by
JAFFE ENTERPRISES
Ron Jaffe

Researched and Edited by Mariah Morgan and Rachel Rutledge

All photos courtesy
AP/ Wide World Photos, Inc.
except the following:
Joe Patronite — Pages 9, 11, 12, 13, 17, 20, 23, 40, 43, 44
The following images are from the collection of Team Stewart:
Sports and Pastimes of American Boys (G. Routledge and Sons, 1884) — Page 14
Sports Illustrated for Kids (©1999) — Page 26
Cycle Sport (©1999 IPC Magazines) — Page 60

Printed in the United States of America

Published by
The Millbrook Press, Inc.
2 Old New Milford Road
Brookfield, Connecticut 06804

www.millbrookpress.com

Library of Congress Cataloging-in-Publication Data

Stewart, Mark.
    Sweet victory: Lance Armstrong's incredible journey, the amazing story of the greatest comeback in
sports / by Mark Stewart
    p.   cm.
    Includes index.
    Summary: The story of the bicyclist who, having won the battle against cancer, went on to win the
world's most grueling bicycle race, the Tour de France.
    ISBN 0-7613-1861-5 (lib. bdg.)   ISBN 0-7613-1387-7 (pbk.)
    1. Armstrong, Lance—Juvenile literature. 2. Cyclists—United States—Biography—Juvenile literature.
3. Tour de France (Bicycle race)—Juvenile literature. [1. Armstrong, Lance. 2. Bicyclists. 3. Tour de
France (Bicycle race)] I. Title.

GV1051.A76 S74 2000
796.6'2'092--dc21
[B]   99-053173

pbk: 1 3 5 7 9 10 8 6 4 2
lib: 3 5 7 9 10 8 6 4 2

CONTENTS

ICE AND LINDA

> *ere were so many*
> *gs he missed out*
> *when he was a kid."*
>
> **KRISTIN ARMSTRONG,**
> **LANCE'S WIFE**

as everything a 17-year-old could hope to be: intelligent, ud, and pretty. She was also pregnant and unmarried, which wanted to be in Plano, Texas, in 1971. On September 17, ity of Dallas and gave birth to a boy she named Lance. chool to take care of Lance. Two years later she married a ng, who adopted the little boy. Father and son never really nce were practically inseparable. Lance was a momma's boy, led all her drive, motivation, and toughness in me," he says. eet in the Armstrong household. Sometimes Linda worked w busy or exhausted she was, she always made sure the time

at his side, through good times and bad.

Triathlete Dave Scott, pictured here winning the 1984 Ironman World Championship, was one of Lance's biggest heroes.

she and her son spent together was "quality time." That meant making sure Lance believed in himself and had a good heart—strengths she knew would enable him to accomplish great things.

Lance was one of those kids who always seemed to be ahead of the pack. He was walking with confidence at nine months and reading aloud by the age of four. He was interested in sports like the other boys in his neighborhood but preferred racing to games like football and baseball. Otherwise, Lance was pretty typical. He did okay in school, got into a little mischief now and then, and liked to hang out with his friends.

As a child, the first organized sport to which Lance was drawn was swimming. He liked to practice, enjoyed being part of a team, and almost always managed to find that little something extra that enabled him to win his heats, even when he went up against older, stronger swimmers. It was something about the atmosphere: the coaches, kids, and parents screaming their heads off, the tension, the cutthroat competition—he was able to take all that emotion and channel it into his performance.

Around the age of nine, Lance became interested in running. By the fifth grade, he was entering long-distance competitions. At first, he jogged along with his mom in 10K events. But soon he was off on his own, sprinting to the front and setting the pace. Lance ran cross-country in junior high and high school, and eventually he added cycling to his repertoire. When he first heard about the triathlon—a sport combining running, swimming, and cycling—he knew he had found his place in the world. To this day, when fans ask him who his cycling heroes were, he politely tells them that he did not have any. "I was a triathlete," he explains, "so I looked up to triathletes like Mark Allen and Dave Scott."

Linda and Lance grew even closer during this period. They seemed to like the same things—sports, Mexican food, rock and roll, and a good laugh. She was her son's biggest supporter and chauffeured him all over the region so he could compete in different events. By the age of 15, Lance was one of the best triathletes in Texas. Lance and friends Chann McRae, Adam Wilk, and John Boggan competed as cross-country runners for East Plano High School, and also entered triathlons together. Each would one day become a professional athlete—McRae and Wilk as cyclists and Boggan as a triathlete.

It was also during this period that Linda's marriage to Terry Armstrong broke up. Once again, it was Lance and Linda, alone against the world.

Champion triathlete Mark Allen was another one of Lance's early sports idols.

WORLD CLASS

"That feeling—the finish line, the last couple of meters— is what motivates me."

LANCE ARMSTRONG

Unlike most sports, where competitors in their teens through mid-20s tend to dominate, triathlon is better suited to athletes in their late 20s through 30s. As triathletes get older, they tend to become stronger and learn to pace themselves better. That is why people in the sport were getting very excited about Lance. By his mid-teens, he was holding his own against mature and experienced competitors and beating many world-class triathletes. The interest and attention only increased when he entered the nationals and won two sprint events.

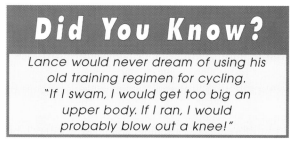

Did You Know?

Lance would never dream of using his old training regimen for cycling. "If I swam, I would get too big an upper body. If I ran, I would probably blow out a knee!"

Unfortunately, Lance's admirers did not include any companies looking to support triathlon. He got frustrated trying to find sponsors. He did not understand why, as his sport's most promising young athlete, no one was willing to invest in his future and

> "It was kind of like an iceberg. You saw this kind of peak, but you knew there was much more below the surface."
>
> CHRIS CHARMICHAEL,
> U.S. NATIONAL CYCLING COACH,
> ON LANCE'S POTENTIAL

help him cover the expenses he incurred while competing. The problem was that there was not a lot of money in the sport to begin with. Eventually, Lance started to lose interest in the triathlon.

At about this time, a man named Chris Charmichael spotted Lance in a competition. Charmichael coached the U.S. cycling team, and he liked the way the young man rode. Lance would either blow everyone away or pull them along until he tired out and they were able to beat him. He was unpolished but very, very exciting. When Lance turned 17, Charmichael's interest turned into an invitation from the United States Cycling Federation to join the Junior National Team. Before he knew it, Lance had ditched triathlon and was competing in international cycling events.

In the spring of 1989, Lance rewarded Charmichael's faith in him when the U.S. team traveled to the Soviet Union for the Junior World Championships. Lance was one of the standouts at the competition and did very well for someone so new to the sport. After he graduated from high school, he continued to compete against the best amateurs in the United States and Europe. Later that year, Lance signed an agreement to ride for the Subaru-Montgomery team, which developed young amateurs and also sponsored a professional racing team. This was exactly the kind of deal he had been looking for when he was a triathlete! Now Lance knew that if he fulfilled his potential as an amateur, he would be offered a chance to turn pro and make a super living from cycling. Salaries for the best riders range between $200,000 and $2 million a year, not including the money they make doing commercials for bicycles and gear.

Switching sports was no big thing for Lance. The object was the same, wasn't it? Push your body and mind to the limit, ignore the pain, and break the tape before anyone else. Basically, Lance loved the rush he felt when he won. "If I could bottle that up and sell it," he says, "I'd be the richest man in the world."

Lance was unusually graceful for someone so new to cycling. His pedal strokes were powerful and sure. He rode with confidence and had a keen competitive spirit. All the running and swimming he had done as a triathlete had helped to strengthen his legs and build his stamina and had taught him to push beyond physical pain and keep going. His upper body was a bit too big for cycling, but there was time to work on that.

The first thing most people noticed about Lance was that he seemed a little different than the other boys in the program. And he was. In the United States, cycling has never been a high-profile sport. Development programs are few and far between; there is no Little League for cycling. Few corporations support the sport with money for training and events, so moms and dads often foot the bills for the expensive bikes, the travel, and the equipment. In most cases, this means the only youngsters that can afford to compete are from well-to-do families. Lance definitely did not come from a wealthy family. Team officials liked that. The cycling world's major criticism of Americans is that they may not be hungry enough. Lance was hungry and highly focused on winning. However, he had nothing to fall back on.

In 1990, Lance decided to move to Austin, Texas. He had access to better training, more interesting people, and, most important, better music. For decades, the Austin music scene has been one of the country's most progressive, with everything from rock to country to jazz to alternative artists. Lance is a major music freak.

In his first full year of cycling, Lance turned in several eye-opening performances, including an 11th-place finish in the individual road race at the World Championships. It was the best finish by a U.S. man in this event since 1977. Not even the great Greg LeMond, America's most famous cyclist, had done that. Lance also won the famous 10-day Bergamasca race in Italy, something no American had done since the 1960s.

Lance moved to Austin in 1990 for two reasons—better training and better music.

Soon, Lance was invited to move up from the junior ranks and join the U.S. national team. It was quite an honor for the 19-year-old. By the conclusion of the 1991 season, Lance had moved to the top of the amateur ranks, winning the U.S. Amateur Championship. He still had a long way to go before turning pro, as his 73rd-place finish in the Tour DuPont—America's biggest race—clearly illustrated. On the other hand, to go from world-class triathlete to world-class cyclist in just two years was a remarkable feat.

Heading into the 1992 season, Lance was determined to have a great year. He wanted to make an impact on the international scene, then turn pro. To do that, he first

Lance rose to international fame riding for the Motorola team.

needed to beat the pros at their own game. Early in the season, Lance entered two United States races that typically were won by professionals: the First Union Grand Prix in Atlanta and the Thrift Drug Classic in Pittsburgh. He won them both. He also finished a respectable 20th against the world's top riders at the summer Olympics in Barcelona, Spain.

Lance's Olympic adventure told him two things: He was good enough to be a professional, and he had nothing more to learn as an amateur. The only difference between himself and the other riders was that they had experience—he certainly felt he was better than 20th! "In Barcelona, I wasn't a professional," he says. "I didn't know where I fit."

Lance stayed in Spain and entered his first race as a pro. The San Sebastian Classic, a one-day event, began in bright sunshine and ended in a driving rain. Of the 111 riders who slogged across the finish line, Lance placed 111th. Short of quitting the race, he could not have done any worse.

Lance (in blue jersey and white helmet) competes at the 1992 Olympics.

A Brief History of Cycling

Who was the first human on two wheels? No one knows for sure, but the idea has definitely been around for a long time. Images of bicycle-like vehicles have been found in Egyptian tombs, and there is a famous stained-glass window in a 375-year-old English church depicting a man on a two-wheeled vehicle.

Literary references to cycling date back three centuries, and there is a detailed account from the 1770s of a wooden horse with two wheels being demonstrated for the queen of France in the courtyard at the palace of Versailles. In the early 1800s, the first bicycle with handlebars, the French *célerifère*, made its debut on the streets of Europe. In 1816 the German *draisine* introduced the concept of a forked front wheel for better steering and handling.

For all their ingenuity, these early attempts lacked one important thing: Riders still had to push themselves along with their feet. Not until a Scottish blacksmith named Macmillan came up with the *dandy horse* in 1839 did a rear crank and primitive pedals first appear. And not until 1855, with the introduction of the French *velocipede*, was anything like a modern bicycle built. This bike's nickname was the "bone rattler." It had wooden wheels and iron tires, with little to cushion the shock between the rump and the road. Ouch!

Fourteen years later, in 1869, the English firm of Reynolds and May displayed a new model called the *ordinary*, which featured rubber tires and a huge front wheel. Needless to say, it was much more comfortable. This basic design of the *ordinary*, though quite dangerous for inexperienced riders, was copied by cycle makers for the next decade.

CYCLING IN THE UNITED STATES

In the 1870s, cycling in the United States received a huge boost thanks to the efforts of Albert Pope, a former military man who was so captivated by this odd contraption that he converted his shoe factory into a bicycle factory in 1878. Pope hired Will Pitman, the country's premier cyclist, to popularize his product, which he christened the *Columbia*. Pitman traveled to New York to demonstrate his cycling skills and was promptly arrested for terrifying the city's horses. Newspapers rallied to Pitman's defense, and his story spread quickly across the country. Thanks to the publicity, Pope soon had bicycle stores in every major city, selling his product for a whopping $150 at a time when a typical American worker was lucky to make more than a dollar or two a day.

At first a pastime for the rich, cycling came within the reach of most Americans by the 1890s, when the price of a new bike dropped to around $50. Those who still could not afford a new model could purchase a used one, or join a cycling club, which lent bikes to its members. The first organized races in the United States were held by these clubs, which boasted thousands of members in the late 1880s and 1890s.

Gone by this time was the dangerous *ordinary* with its gigantic front wheel, replaced by the *rover* "safety bicycle," which featured two wheels of roughly identical size. Meanwhile, saddles were getting more comfortable, and the new location of the seat—between the wheels on a triangular frame—also made for a less jarring ride.

THE NEED FOR SPEED

The first recorded bicycle race took place outside of Paris, in 1868. By the 1890s, major road races were being held in every large city on both sides of the Atlantic. Some drew more than 15,000 fans. In the middle of the decade, cycling was unchallenged as the world's most popular sport. Between prize money and sponsorship deals, the top professional riders earned $10,000 a year and more—a staggering amount in those days.

Cycling remained an immensely popular sport in Europe, but in the United States interest began to decline in the early years of the 20th century. A race tactic called "bottling"—where two riders worked as a team, with one sprinting out in the lead and the other blocking his pursuers—seemed unfair to fans, and they abandoned the sport.

Just as damaging was America's budding love affair with the motor car. Many fans of high-speed sports soon began to view cycling as primitive. By 1910 major road races in the United States were rare; the once mighty bicycle had become little more than a "poor man's" mode of transportation. What remained of the sport usually took place on indoor tracks, or "velodromes."

In Europe, however, cycling remained strong. The Tour de France, launched in 1903, was the ultimate test of speed, skill, and endurance, and remains so to this day. A rider must be in terrific shape just to finish; to win, he must be a member of a highly organized and dedicated team. Other events range from single-day competitions to stage races of a week or more, and make up pro cycling's "season," which now stretches from the early spring to the late fall.

CYCLING TODAY

Today, cycling is the major summer sport in several countries, including France, Belgium, Holland, and Italy. Its stars are as well known to European sports fans as the top major-league baseball players are to American fans. Since the 1950s, major corporations have poured money into the sport for publicity and prestige. They own teams and hire the top "free agents," just as American sports teams do.

During the 20th century, there have been scores of super cyclists hailing from a dozen or so different countries. The most famous include Frenchmen Louison Bobet, Jacques Anquetil, and Bernard Hinault, Belgian Eddie Merckx, and Spaniard Miguel Indurain.

Lance Armstrong was hardly the first big-name American. Prior to World War II, the United States produced three dominant riders: August Zimmerman, Bobby Walthour, and Major Taylor, the first African-American athlete in any sport to become an international star. In the 1980s, Greg LeMond burst onto the racing scene and won the Tour de France three times. Given the on-again off-again popularity of American cycling over the past 100 years, the United States has more than distinguished itself on the international racing scene.

As for the future of cycling, it appears to be in fine shape. The sport is virtually unchallenged in Europe during the summer season, and fans cannot seem to get enough of it. In the United States, cycling's fate depends on how much money it can raise to attract and develop young riders. Athletes like Lance, it is hoped, will open the country's eyes to the high drama and spectacle of the sport.

With a little more money, a bit more publicity, and a break here and there, the 21st century could be a special one for cycling in the United States!

EUROPEAN INVASION

chapter 3

"I'm not the next Greg LeMond. I'm the first Lance Armstrong."

LANCE ARMSTRONG

There are two ways to look at a last-place finish. Either someone is trying to tell you something (like "You stink!"), or you have nowhere to go but up. Given the conditions of the race, and the excitement he felt about being a brand-new pro, Lance realized it was a minor victory just to finish the San Sebastian

Classic. That is the kind of person he is. He is not a bit shy, nor does he lack confidence. That is why, two weeks after the San Sebastian disaster, Lance entered his next race with his chin up and his chest out.

The event was an important World Cup race, held high in the mountains around Zurich, Switzerland. Every top

Did You Know?

After finishing 111th at San Sebastian, Lance called his mother and asked if she thought he had made a mistake turning pro. Not on your life, she replied. She told him to suck it up and get back on the bike. That was all Lance needed to hear. The rest is history.

pro in the sport was there. Despite the odds against Lance, at the end of the race it was he who flashed across the finish line in second place. It was preposterous to think that this unknown American, this "baby," could have wiped out so many top riders in such

Lance strains for speed during his time trail at the 1992 Tour DuPont.

a huge race. No one knew what to make of Lance Armstrong. Who was he? Where did he come from?

Most perplexing to European fans was why this upstart Texan did not seem satisfied with second place. As far as they were concerned, his performance was a miracle, a one-in-a-million, once-in-a-lifetime finish. In Lance's mind, however, coming in second meant he had still been beaten. "I define success as winning races," he explains.

Lance returned to Austin and began preparing for the 1993 cycling season. He came out flying that spring, ready to take on the world. He did not care that it was his first full year as a pro. Lance felt he was ready to make an impact, and he believed the other riders on his team (now sponsored by Motorola) were ready to kick some butt, too.

Normally, it takes a young rider a few years before people start to notice him, but no one ever accused Lance of being normal. He won the Thrift Drug Classic for the second time, as well as the two other races in the Thrift series, to win a $1 million bonus, which was split up among the members of the Motorola team. The last of the three races was the U.S. Pro Championship, so Lance was not only making big bucks, but he was also the national champion.

In the Tour DuPont, Lance turned in another startling performance against the world's best riders, finishing second. He was in position to win as the race entered its next-to-last day, but he failed to pull away from 29-year-old Mexican star Raul Alcala as they struggled through the mountains of North Carolina. The final stage, a

Lance exults as he crosses the finish line first in the 1993 Tour de France.
He shocked the cycling world by winning the race's eighth stage.

36.5-mile (58.8-km) time trial, was perfectly suited for the lightning-fast Alcala, who ended up beating Lance by two minutes.

This time Lance was a bit more diplomatic about his fine finish. He told reporters it was the greatest accomplishment of his young career, though mainly because he got to lead a team for the first time. Lance was the point man for the Motorola squad while team leader Andy Hampsten was competing at a Swiss event. Needless to say, the folks at Motorola were very pleased with the results. "This was more than just finishing second," Lance says. "I led a team, and that's something 21-year-old 'neo-pros' aren't supposed to do."

Less than two months later, Lance was in his first Tour de France, the world's biggest cycling event. In Europe, cycling is as big as football is in the United States And the Tour de France is the Super Bowl of cycling. It is a three-week race covering about 2,300 miles (3,700 km). Divided into a series of daily stages, the Tour is designed to test all of a rider's physical and mental abilities. Some regard it as the most challenging event in all of sports. Winning this race requires every bit of skill and luck a rider can muster. Just winning a single stage is a cause for celebration. Greg LeMond, who won the race an amazing three times, was the only American to win the Tour de France since it began in 1903.

Did You Know?

Although Lance recommends all young riders wear protective helmets, he believes pros should not be required to do so. "I try to wear mine as much as possible, but we're all adults, and all professionals, and I think it should be left up to the rider to decide."

More than a dozen teams enter the Tour de France. Riders work together to put their top man in front and then employ various strategies to keep him there. Naturally, first-time riders are expected to support their teammates, keep their eyes open, and learn. That is just what Lance did. During the first seven stages, he concentrated on doing his best and keeping the team competitive. But during the Tour's eighth stage, he felt a surge of confidence and energy. He decided to put everything he had into his ride that day and surprised the leaders by turning in the top time. Once again, European fans were dumbfounded. The kid won a stage? Impossible!

*Lance acknowledges the thunderous ovation after winning the 1993
World Championship in Oslo, Norway.*

Impossible, maybe, but true. Only two cyclists younger than Lance had ever won a stage of the Tour de France. Those who had considered Lance's second-place finish at the big 1992 race in Zurich a fluke were now starting to take him seriously. No, he was not ready to win the Tour de France, but certainly his future was very bright.

Lance performed well in the ninth stage, but by the 10th and 11th stages, he was beginning to tire. By the start of the 12th stage, he was exhausted and trailing leader Miguel Indurain by 55 minutes. Rather than risk an injury, Motorola team manager Jim Ochowicz decided to pull his young star out of the race.

After a brief recovery period, Lance got back on the European circuit and continued to learn and improve. By the end of the season, he was in top form. At the World Championships in Oslo, Norway, Lance had the ride of his life. He outpedaled the sport's biggest names—including the favorite, Indurain—to score an unbelievable win. The key was a stunning performance on a rain-soaked day when the others merely hoped to stay on their bikes. Riding on pure emotion, Lance gritted his teeth and exploded away from the pack to open up an insurmountable lead.

Lance was the second-youngest rider ever to win this event. He went into the winter off-season as the proud owner of the famous rainbow-striped jersey, which says to everyone in cycling, "I am the world champion!"

That winter, the world champion could walk down any street in America and go completely unnoticed. That was how little sports fans in this country knew about pro cycling! This did not bother Lance. In fact, he rather enjoyed it. He maintained his privacy and was able to stick to his training routine. Had a European rider won,

Did You Know?

After Lance won the World Championship in 1993, he was to meet Norway's King Harald V. When he was told his mother could not come along, he turned down the monarch's invitation, nearly causing an international incident. "You don't check your mother at the door," he kept saying. When Harald heard that this young man wanted to share his greatest moment with his mom, he could not refuse. So Lance and Linda got the royal treatment. "I think the king thought it was cool," he says.

the scene would have been very different. "These other guys that wear the rainbow jersey are gods in their respective countries," he says. "They spend the majority of their off-season flying here and there, doing commercial this and commercial that, and they forget about their biking."

Lance had Viatcheslav Ekimov (center) in his sights at the 1994 Tour DuPont but could not catch him in the end.

The 1994 season got in gear for Lance with a series of U.S. races, including the Thrift Drug Classic, which he won for the third consecutive year. At the Tour DuPont, Lance had leader Viatcheslav Ekimov in his sights the entire race but just could not catch him. For the second time in a row, Lance finished second. He learned a good lesson about strategy: Even when you feel stronger than the man in front of you, sometimes that is not enough. "When two riders are strong, it becomes a cat-and-mouse game," says Lance. This time, the mouse got away.

Lance was beginning to realize that being world champion had its drawbacks. All through the Tour DuPont, Ekimov was talking about what it would take to beat Lance, and how Lance was the only person he worried about. A year earlier, Ekimov probably did not know who Lance was. "It's not an easy jersey to wear," Lance says of the rainbow-colored shirt. "I felt like a marked man."

Lance also recognized that despite the honor of being world champion, he was nowhere near the top of his sport. In order to take that major step, he had to make a major decision. He would have to live in Europe during the racing season. He purchased a home in Milan, Italy, for his new base of operations.

Lance scored no major victories in 1994. He finished out the season with a seventh-place showing at the World Championships. It was almost a relief to relinquish the rainbow jersey—finally he could look forward to running a race without being the target of every other rider.

Not until that winter did he realize what a special thing it was. "When I won the jersey it was a surprise," he says. "I took it and wore it for a year and you don't realize at a young age, at a young point in your career, what you have. Then when you lose the jersey and you see another person wearing it, you realize exactly what it was that you achieved. And what an honor it was."

Lance, riding here in Italy, got to wear the rainbow jersey throughout the 1994 season.

STARS AND STRIPES

chapter **4**

> *"I have to carry the sport in this country, and the best way to do that is to win and win big."*
>
> **LANCE ARMSTRONG**

ance began 1995 feeling he was ready to make that big leap into the top level of cycling. That meant the Motorola team would have to be at its best. Although cycling seems like an individual sport, no individual can win a major competition without a good team behind him. If it were up to a lone rider to stay ahead all day, he would become mentally and physically exhausted. But working as part of a team, a "hot" rider can be protected, pulled along, and then put in position to break away and win.

For Lance, the first order of business in 1995 was to stop finishing second in the Tour DuPont and win the darn thing. After all, how seriously would Europe take a cyclist who could not even win the big event in his own country? This would not be easy. The Motorola team

> *"In Europe, he already rides on so much emotion, and that is why he's so strong. Bring him here, in front of the home fans, and he will be almost unbeatable."*
>
> **PASCAL HERVE, ON LANCE'S CHANCES AT THE 1996 OLYMPICS**

Cycling legends Bernard Hinault (left) and Eddy Merckx

took longer to come together than in previous years, and manager Jim Ochowicz did not feel he had the right mix of riders until just before the 1,130-mile (1,819-km) race.

That mix included teammate Andrea Peron, an Italian who had finished third behind Lance in this race in 1993 and 1994. In the early stages of the Tour DuPont, when defending champ Viatcheslav Ekimov attempted to take the lead, it was Peron who caught up to him and kept him from opening a huge gap. Eventually, Ekimov got tired and drifted back to the pack. For a while, Peron was the race leader, but after the fourth stage he began to fade and Lance took charge. Finally, it was Lance's turn to take command. When the only remaining threat—defending World Cup champ Gianluca Bortolami—wiped out on a patch of slick pavement, Lance pumped hard through the mountains and completely dominated the remainder of the race. Finally, he was Tour DuPont champion. Without Peron's early work, however, the outcome might have been very different.

Lance next set his sights on the Tour de France. Miguel Indurain, at the height of his powers, was the overwhelming favorite to do something no one had ever done before: win a record fifth Tour in a row. Only three other riders—Eddy Merckx, Bernard Hinault, and Jacques Anquetti—had won five, and no one had ever won six. Lance knew he was still too inexperienced to win (in two tries he had yet to even finish), but

LANCE ARMSTRONG

Sports Illustrated KIDS

CYCLIST ◆ AUSTIN, TEXAS

Trading cards of cyclists were not very popular until Lance started making headlines. This SI for Kids card is now one of the sport's hottest collectibles.

he definitely wanted to make it to the end and perhaps even win a stage. Besides Indurain, Lance would have to outpedal superstars Tony Rominger, Gianni Bugno, Piotr Ugrumov, Richard Virenque, Marco Pantani, and Eugeni Berzin.

Against this lot, Lance's chances were only fair. He had worked hard to improve in the time trial stages, where riders compete against the clock instead of one another. But this was the specialty of Indurain and Rominger. Winning a stage in the mountains seemed out of the question, too. Indurain was strong in the uphill stretches, as were Berzin and Virenque. Lance, at 5 feet 10 (178 cm) and 175 pounds (79 kg), had too much weight to carry up and down the Alps and Pyrenees.

As the race unfolded, Indurain opened up a good lead and maintained it right to the finish. Lance did well, too. He completed the race for the first time and did indeed win a stage. But he will always remember the 1995 Tour de France with great sadness and despair. His teammate, Fabio Casartelli, lost control of his bike and fell in the mountains and died of severe head trauma. "To lose a teammate," says Lance, "was the hardest moment in my career."

Casartelli was buried two days later. At the funeral, Lance vowed to a friend that he would win a stage for Fabio. The next day, near the conclusion of the 18th stage, Lance was riding in a pack with about a dozen others. Normally, there is a wild sprint when the finish line is sighted, and the winner is often decided by a matter of inches. Lance was not much good in these sprints, so he decided to make an unorthodox move. With 18 miles (29 km) to go, he caught everyone by surprise when he suddenly broke away from the pack. It took the other riders several minutes to figure out how to respond to this challenge, and by then Lance was gone. With 6 miles (10 km) left he was almost a minute ahead of the next rider. "I had a feeling nobody would react," he says.

A few hundred feet before Lance streaked across the finish line, he let go of the handle bars, pointed to the sky and blew kisses toward the heavens. European fans generally dislike this kind of gesture, and for this reason Lance was never a favorite early in his career the way Greg LeMond was. But this time the fans knew Lance was not showing off. "I was only trying to recognize Fabio," he says, adding that thinking of his fallen teammate gave him the strength to win the 103-mile (166-km) stage. "The last few kilometers I started to suffer, but I had Fabio on my mind the whole time. There's no doubt there were four feet on the pedals that day."

When Lance finished the Tour de France, it was one of the proudest moments in his life. Next, he went to San Sebastian and improved on his 111th-place finish four years earlier by winning the 1995 event handily. It marked the first time an American had ever captured a World

Lance points skyward in honor of his fallen teammate, Fabio Casartelli, as he crosses the finish line first in the 18th stage of the 1995 Tour de France.

Cup event. At season's end, Lance was being mentioned among the sport's elite. *Velonews*, one of cycling's leading international publications, named him Male Cyclist of the Year.

The 1996 season brought more success. In April and May, he won Belgium's prestigious Fleche Wallone Classic and scored second-place finishes in six other big races. At the end of May, Lance entered and won the Tour DuPont again. He led pretty much

Did You Know?

Lance took some of the money he made in his great 1995 season and sponsored a nationwide junior Olympic race series, which introduced cycling to thousands of young boys and girls.

wire-to-wire, bringing American cycling into the spotlight for the first time since the glory days of LeMond. An estimated two million people lined the roads to cheer Lance as he whizzed past, and a huge crowd was on hand as he rolled across the finish line more than 3 minutes ahead of the second-place rider. European spectators marveled at the reception American fans gave their newest hero. Cycling was not dead in America. Thanks to this charismatic, young champion, it was very much alive and well.

And Lance aimed to keep it that way. With the Olympics set for that summer in Atlanta, he had set his sights on winning a gold medal on his "home turf" with the whole world watching. So intent was Lance on this goal that he decided to use the Tour de France as a "training race" for the Olympics, which started just 10 days after the Tour. He took a month off, then entered the Tour to work on getting back in shape.

Lance's decision was not popular with the people who run the pro cycling world. They felt the Tour de France was 10 times more prestigious than the Olympics. But

there were other forces at work that gave the Summer Games special importance. Team sponsor Motorola announced that 1996 would be its final year in cycling. Lance was afraid that the sport would take a big step back-

All-time great Greg LeMond (left) is one of Lance's biggest fans and greatest friends.

Lance grabs a snack on his way to winning the 1996 Tour DuPont.
Two million people lined the roads to cheer him on.

ward in the United States if his team were disbanded, and he did not wish to sign with a European team. In LeMond's heyday, he rode for a French team, which limited his appeal to sports fans in the United States. A gold medal might reverse Motorola's decision or at least attract another high-profile American sponsor to the sport. By winning the Olympics, Lance believed he could help American cycling take a step forward instead of a step back. "You can win World Cup races, you can win the Tour de France, but in this country people don't remember those things," he explains. "The Olympic Games—that's what sticks with the American people."

OH, MY GOD, I AM GOING TO DIE

chapter 5

"After I found out, I didn't care about cycling. It was the worst fear I'd ever experienced."

LANCE ARMSTRONG

The 138-mile (222-km) road race at the 1996 Olympics wound its way through the outskirts of Atlanta, in the city's fashionable Buckhead neighborhood. Lance was not only the favorite to win, he was the crowd favorite, too. He saw fans waving Texas state flags, and he rode over orange longhorns (a symbol of the Lone Star State) painted on the pavement as a show of support. During the 14th lap, Lance tried to pull away from the pack but drew an immediate crowd. Everyone in the race knew he was the man to beat, so no one was about to let him just pedal away with the gold medal.

> ### Did You Know?
>
> Weeks prior to his cancer diagnosis, Lance made two major moves. The first was a move into his new house on Lake Austin. The second was a move to Cofidis, one of the top French racing teams.

Though he tried his best, Lance could not keep up this pace. With three laps remaining, he began to fade. When the leaders whirred past the finish line, Lance was nowhere in sight, finishing 12th—a minute and a half behind. "I took the attack," Lance remembers. "But it's hard to break away from a group like that. That's what it's

Lance was the man to beat at the 1996 Olympics. Despite leading the race early, he fell far back in the pack. Something was not right.

about, taking risks. Sometimes they work, sometimes they don't. I've done that move a lot before, and it's worked."

Lance could say whatever he wanted, but everyone knew he should have blown the other riders away. Something was wrong. He was not feeling well. A few weeks earlier, doctors had prescribed antibiotics for a nasty case of strep throat and slight bronchitis, but he did not want to take them so close to the Olympics. Lance felt weak heading into the Summer Games. After the race, he blamed his lack of stamina on not being 100 percent.

A few weeks later, on the evening of October 2, Lance coughed up some blood and felt severe pain in one of his testicles. There had been a small bump on it for at least three years, but he had never mentioned it to anyone because it never hurt this much before. Besides, cyclists are trained to ignore discomfort. Lance simply assumed it was related to spending too many hours on a bicycle seat.

Well, it wasn't. He had cancer. Worse, in the years he had ignored the swelling, the cancer had spread to his lungs, his abdomen, and his brain. Lance had a dozen tumors in his chest and two lesions in his head. This was not good. His chances for survival were less than 50–50. The testicle was removed by doctors immediately. "I thought the same thing everybody thinks when they hear the word 'cancer,'" says Lance. "I thought, 'Oh, my God, I am going to die.'"

As soon as he left the hospital, Lance got on the Internet and starting learning all he could about the causes and cures for his kind of cancer. His mother moved in with him, and the two of them searched the Web frantically for new information. Lance treated his disease like a racecourse. He wanted to learn everything there was to learn about

Did You Know?

Years ago, Lance's cancer would have been untreatable. Brian Piccolo, a star running back for the Chicago Bears, died of the same illness in 1970.

cancer. He wanted to know what to expect, what his options were, and he wanted to know who knew more than anyone else.

He soon discovered a doctor at the Indiana University Medical Center named Lawrence Einhorn. Dr. Einhorn and his colleague, Dr. Craig Nichols, had perfected a treatment for testicular cancer. Lance met with them and explained that he wanted to beat this disease, but he also wanted to race again.

Dr. Craig Nichols joins Lance at a press conference three years after the bicycle racer was diagnosed with cancer. Special treatments developed by Dr. Nichols enabled Lance to race again.

Everything but the brain cancer would probably respond to chemotherapy, they told Lance. "Chemo" is a treatment that floods the body with special medicine that kills cancer cells. For some reason it does not always work on cells growing in the brain. Brain cancer is usually treated with doses of radiation, but this was not an option for Lance. Radiation therapy can leave patients with a slight loss of balance, and for a world-class cyclist this is the equivalent of a death sentence. Because the tumors were in a part of Lance's brain that could be easily reached by surgeons, the decision was made to risk an operation. On October 24, 1996, a medical team opened Lance's brain and cut out the two lesions. He still feels weird when he thinks about it. "They lifted my skull out"—Lance grimaces—"like you'd cut the top off a pumpkin."

For Lance's chemo, the doctors decided not to use Bleomycin, the drug most often prescribed in these circumstances. Bleomycin tends to reduce a patient's breathing capacity, which would also have ruined any chance of a comeback for Lance. Instead, a drug called Ifosfomide was used. Ifosfomide is just as effective as Bleomycin but causes patients to become violently ill. Lance felt the short-term pain was worth the long-term gain.

Every two-and-a-half weeks, for three months, Lance underwent five days of chemotherapy. His hair fell out, and he lost 20 pounds (9 kg)—almost all of it muscle. He felt horrible. And he was never sure if he would make it. In the beginning, Lance thought that he could use his athletic training to endure this miserable treatment. He soon realized that beating cancer has nothing to do with who you are or what you do. Often it's just dumb luck.

Lance, pictured here in March 1997, looked thin and tired after his chemotherapy treatments.

After each treatment Lance would return to Austin and get right back on his bike.
His dream was to suit up and race again one day.

ROAD TO RECOVERY

"I might have a bald head and might not be as fast, but I'll be out there. I'm going to race again."

LANCE ARMSTRONG

To keep from going crazy between chemotherapy sessions, Lance would hop on his bike and take a (for him) leisurely 20-mile (32-km) ride around Austin. Sometimes he did not make it home. More than once he was discovered gasping for air on a stranger's front lawn.

Lance had a lot of time to think on these rides. He thought about how he had lived his life in the past, and how he would live it differently if he survived. He also thought about what he would like to accomplish in the unlikely event that he was able to return to the world of pro cycling. And even though Lance tried not to think about it, he sometimes wondered what it would be like to die.

Lance got plenty of encouragement from the other cancer patients he met. He saw incredible courage in the faces of children that made him search for something extra within himself. Eventually, he found it. It was not something he had learned as a triathlete or a cyclist. It was something strong and wonderful that had been in him all along. Then something strange happened. Other patients started looking to Lance for that strength. He did not fully understand it, but he liked it.

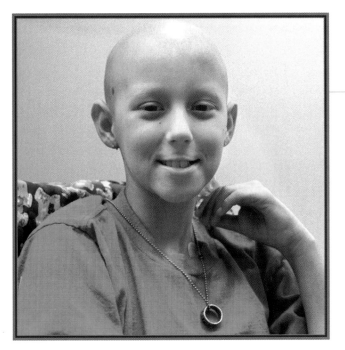

Fellow survivor Kelly Davidson was one of the many kids Lance met while undergoing chemotherapy in 1996 and 1997.

When Lance looked back on his life, he did have a couple of regrets. His biggest one was that he never met someone he wanted to marry. As so often happens in these circumstances, that person came into his life when he was feeling lowest. Her name was Kristin Richard. Lance had hired her to help market a benefit bicycle race he was organizing.

Kristin struck up a friendship with Lance during the last part of his chemotherapy treatment. He sure didn't look like much. Lance's hair and eyebrows had fallen out, he bore ugly brown scars from his chemo, and he looked like he had been starved and beaten. Still, Kristin could tell the fire was still burning inside of him. It would be a shame, she thought, if the flame were snuffed out. Lance seemed like a terrific guy.

Lance survived the radical chemo treatments, and eventually he started feeling better. He and Kristin grew closer and saw as much of each other as they could. More good news came in the spring of 1997. The tumors in Lance's lungs no longer appeared on his chest X ray. In October there was even better news. A test revealed that Lance's HCG count—which measures the presence of cancer in the blood—was down to 1.5.

"I met Lance at the tail end of his treatment. So I met him when he had no hair, no eyebrows, nothing. He was kind of quiet, withdrawn, and pale. So different than the person you see today, yet really not different in so many ways."
KRISTIN ARMSTRONG

When he started treatment, the number was 100,000. Technically, this meant Lance was cancer-free.

Lance had a second chance, and he aimed to make the most of it. He was healthy and happy and more focused than ever. As he slowly brought his body back to life, he noticed something interesting. During his illness, Lance had lost almost all of his upper-body muscle. It would only take a few months to build back up again, the doctors assured him. But he did not want to build those muscles up—for a cyclist, losing 10 to 15 pounds (4.5 to 6.8 kg) of upper-body muscle is like a gift from the gods. In a mountain race like the Tour de France, for instance, shedding that extra weight might make the difference between first place and 50th. There are no pills and no special diets that can do this for a rider—ironically, about the only thing that would work is something as devastating as chemo. "Why not make the most out of a horrible experience?" Lance thought. "Why not rebuild my body so that it's absolutely perfect for cycling?"

And that is exactly what he did. The 20-mile (32-km) rides became 50-mile (80-km) rides. Then 100-mile (161-km) rides. Over the next few months, he developed the muscles in his legs until they were like steel bands, while carefully strengthening his arms, shoulders, and chest without adding any bulk.

In August, Lance was told by cycling sponsor Cofidis that they were dropping him from the team. He already had an advanced case of cancer when he signed with them a year earlier, the company claimed, so they were not obligated to continue paying him. "No problem," was Lance's response. "If I come back, I want it to be for a team that wants me."

That team turned out to be the one sponsored by the U.S. Postal Service. Impressed by Lance's continuing recovery, they signed him up. If nothing else, it seemed to be a good public-relations move. Little did team officials expect that by January 1998 he would be one of the best riders in camp. And Lance knew he could be much, much better. He had rebuilt his body for racing but had yet to get his stamina back. "My lack of fitness gnawed at me," he remembers.

Lance gnawed right back. Enlisting his old coach, Chris Charmichael, and longtime friend Bob Roll, Lance relocated to the mountains of North Carolina and began training on the same roads that had taken him to glory twice as winner of the Tour DuPont. Charmichael would work on Lance's body, while the upbeat Roll would work on his mind. In seven days, Lance and Roll covered 800 of the most mountainous miles

When Lance signed to race for the U.S. Postal Service, no one—not even "teammates" Kristin and Linda—could have imagined how well he would do.

(1,288 km) east of the Mississippi. Lance emerged with a whole new outlook. He stopped thinking about what could have been, and all the bad things that had happened, and found a new reason to ride. He was no longer Lance Armstrong, former champion; he was now Lance Armstrong, cancer survivor. This was what he needed to make his comeback really mean something. The spark was back. Lance was ready to begin his climb back to the top.

Lance's first race was the Ruta del Sol, an eight-day event that attracted a handful of top riders. Lance finished 15th. He never felt so good about a 15th-place finish in

Two of the greatest names in cycling—Greg LeMond (center) and Miguel Indurain (right)—join Lance for a 1998 charity exhibition race in Austin, Texas.

his life! He tried some more events but did not do as well. In the seven-day Paris-Nice event, he realized the first day he did not have it, so he quit and flew back home to Austin to work on his stamina.

On May 24, 1998, a small item appeared in newspapers around the world. Most people missed it; it was buried in the back of the sports section, near the box scores and transactions. It reported that Lance Armstrong, the promising cyclist struck down in his prime by cancer, had stunned spectators in his hometown of Austin by winning the Sprint 56K Criterium. With half a lap to go, he broke away from a group that included top riders Todd Littlehales and Chann McRae, and sprinted to victory. Lance downplayed the win, which caused many in the crowd to weep with joy. "It's not a stage in the Tour de France," he cautioned reporters.

Tour de France? Who said anything about the Tour de France? Was Lance Armstrong actually thinking about entering that race again?

No. He hoped to *win* it.

The Long and
Winding Road

In the sport of cycling, road races come in all shapes and sizes. As a rule, they cover anywhere from 20 to 3,000 miles (32 to 4,830 km), and can take less than an hour or more than two weeks. In multiple-stage races, such as the Tour de France, all the riders start together each morning. Depending on how quickly they finish that day's stage, they either pick up or lose seconds. The first cyclists to cross the finish line generally receive a "bonus" of a few precious seconds. The winner of each stage typically receives a trophy or prize money. For these reasons, each stage always ends in a mad dash to the finish.

Cycling is different from other long-distance sports in that teamwork is necessary to win. A team's top rider must be sheltered from the wind by his teammates in order to conserve his energy, and it is up to team members to catch up to rivals who attempt to break away from the pack and "bring them back." At the conclusion of a race, or at the end of a stage, a team's lead rider—still fresh and full of energy—sprints out and tries to finish first. His teammates, meanwhile, can try to buy him time by blocking the pack.

Each stage of a long race is full of strategy and drama. There are attacks, counterattacks, breakaways, and chases. Sometimes, rivals come together to form their own pack, each believing he has what it takes to beat the others in a late-race duel. Occasionally, a team decides to switch its leader and begins sheltering a rider it feels has a better chance of winning.

I CAN DO THIS

chapter 7

"What he's doing now is a huge accomplishment. It would be unfair to expect more."

POSTAL SERVICE TEAM DIRECTOR MARK GORSKI

History will remember the words of those who thought Lance would never come all the way back. And it will record his victories along the way. But the race that cycling people will cherish most is one that history may forget. It occurred the first week in June 1998, at the U.S. Pro Cycling Championships in Philadelphia—the sport's richest one-day event. It would have been the perfect place for Lance to burst back onto the scene. But he was not the only rider who needed a win.

A year earlier, while Lance was still recovering from chemo, his old Motorola teammate, George Hincapie, was the top American finisher in the race and therefore the U.S. pro champ. An hour later he was stripped of this honor on a technicality. Lance read about the incident and felt terrible for Hincapie, who had supported Lance in many a race over the years.

*George Hincapie (left) and Lance worked well together in 1998.
With Lance's help, Hincapie won the U.S. Pro Cycling title.*

Now it was time to repay the favor and right a year-old wrong. Early in the race, a group of five riders broke from the pack and managed to stay in front for nearly four hours. Lance knew what he had to do. He put everything he had into a mad sprint, and the pack followed him as he closed ground on the leaders. With 16 miles (26 km) to go, he passed the lead group and took the lead himself. He pushed the pace and ran down others who tried to break away, while Hincapie stayed back and conserved his energy. With just a few miles to go, Lance led his teammate through the pack and into the lead. Once Hincapie established himself in front, Lance dropped back, exhausted. The record books credit the win to Hincapie and give Lance a 33rd-place finish.

Everyone on the team knew what had really happened. And no one would forget.

A week later it was Lance's turn for a little glory when he entered the four-day Tour de Luxembourg. All eyes were on Lance when the first stage started. When the first

Lance's fourth-place finish at the 1998 World Championship was a major step in his incredible comeback.

stage ended, all eyes were on Lance again. After a dramatic one-on-one duel with Lauri Aus, he pulled away to finish first. Over the next three days, Lance was able to maintain his lead and won by more than three minutes.

The rest of the 1998 season was like a fairy tale for Lance, as he won two more major races, and recorded Top 5 finishes in four other European events—including fourth in the grueling Tour of Spain and fourth at the World Championships. It exceeded even his wildest dreams. "After I came back to Europe the only goal I set for myself was to finish every race I entered," he says. "To do well in the world championship is something I would have never believed possible."

Lance spent the winter of 1998–1999 focusing on what he needed to do win the Tour de France. What eight months earlier had seemed like a crazy dream was now a real possibility. Lance had become a better rider in all the ways that make a difference in an event like the Tour. The biggest difference would come in the torturous mountain stages. Lance had always been a good climber, but day after exhausting day in the Alps and Pyrenees simply wore him out. Now, however, he weighed under 160 pounds (73 kg), which meant he would be pulling 15 to 20 pounds (7 to 9 kg) less up those steep slopes. In a race where seconds can decide each stage, this gave Lance an important edge.

In preparation for the 1999 season, Lance tested his bike at Texas A&M in College Station, Texas. A&M has one of only three wind tunnels built specifically for cycling. John Cobb, who designed and built Lance's bike, was on hand to watch the tests and made key adjustments to the front fork, handlebars, and wheels. He also repositioned Lance to create less wind resistance. Lance had first used the wind tunnel in 1991, at the suggestion of Greg LeMond, and he has been back many times since.

Lance's home state of Texas also provided him with a good workout environment to prepare for the blustery days riders sometimes encounter during the Tour. European events often feature strong winds. In South Texas, strong winds are a way life. "It's a south wind in the summer and a north wind in the winter, so there's no way around it," says Lance. "Either time of year you're fighting the weather. Absolutely it helped. It's very windy in Europe all the time."

THE ARMSTRONG FILE

LANCE'S FAVORITE...

Food He Eats During Races
Pasta, Cereal, and Bread

Food He Eats in Training
Salad, Grilled Veggies

**Food He Loves,
But Is "Forbidden" to Eat**
Burgers, Fries, and Ice Cream

Favorite Hobby
Computers
"I'm an Internet junkie. In most races I have my laptop with me."

Favorite Athlete
Fellow Cyclist Miguel Indurain
"I'm a big fan of Big Mig."

During his races early in 1999, Lance usually finished with the pack, winning a stage here and there, but mostly keeping a low profile. Of course, he always made sure to work on the skills he would need for the Tour de France. Lance flew to France more than a month before the Tour so he could work out in the Alps and Pyrenees, and also compete in tune-up events. He concentrated on climbing and also tinkered with his technique on flat stretches. He performed particularly well in the mountains during two June races. Still, no one considered him a threat to take the Tour de France.

By July 3, Lance was ready for the big race. The opening day of the Tour de France was a "prologue" course through the remote back roads of western France. The early

"Actually, I can thank my illness for losing the body fat. I'm close to 20 pounds lighter because of the illness. When I was sick, I lost all of my muscle and was able to build back the body in a different way."

LANCE ARMSTRONG

stages of the race tend to favor the sprinters, and this was no exception. Lance and 179 other riders took off from the town of Montaigu and went all-out for 5 miles (8 km). Lance completed the course in 8 minutes, 2 seconds—7 seconds ahead of runner-up Alex Zulle—for an average speed of 31 miles (50 km) per hour. Not bad for a guy who was supposed to be dead! Lance's victory was the first ever for the Postal Service team in the Tour de France. He received a 20-second bonus for his stage win, putting him 27 seconds in front. It also earned him the fabled yellow jersey, which is worn only by the leader of the Tour de France.

Lance's win made headlines around the world. It also gave the race a big boost at just the right time. Cycling had received a black eye while he was away, as many top teams were found to be administering performance-enhancing drugs to their riders. Wherever investigators looked, they seemed to find evidence of drug use. At the 1998 Tour de France, nine riders were expelled during the race for failing drug tests, and rumors abounded that dozens more had found ways to beat the Tour's screenings for banned substances. Before Lance won the first stage, the main topic of conversation among fans and the press concerned which riders might be on drugs this year. In other words, the Tour de France was in danger of becoming a big joke.

Now everyone was interested in Lance. It still seemed absurd to believe he was strong enough to challenge the world's top riders, but at least it was an upbeat story. As the international news media crowded around Lance, he answered questions about his illness, his comeback, and his performance that day. Little did reporters know that they would be seeing a lot more of this remarkable young man in the days to come.

Team strategy is everything in the Tour de France. After Lance's unexpected win, Postal Service team officials were quick to point out that they would not let their riders kill themselves to win the upcoming series of sprints. Lance and his teammates would save their energy for the mountains. Yes, they were pleased he was wearing the yellow jersey, but they would not risk everything to defend it.

The first official stage of the race covered 129 miles (208 km) of relatively flat ground. Lance maintained an excellent pace to finish with a huge pack of riders battling to cross the line first. That gave him a good enough time to keep the yellow jersey for another day. The Tour's second stage, a 109-mile (175-km) sprint, saw Lance drop to second, behind Estonian rider Jaan Kirispuu. Lance was counting his blessings, however, after learning that three of the Tour's top riders—Zulle, Ivan Gotti, and Michael Boogerd—wiped out on the treacherous Passage du Gois causeway in the port city of St. Nazaire. Zulle had lost 6 minutes, which meant he would have to really push himself to get back among the leaders.

Lance could hardly believe he was in first place after the first day of the 1999 Tour de France. He became the first member of the U.S. Postal Service team ever to win a stage of the race.

Lance signs autographs for French fans from the team trailer during the 1999 Tour de France.

Lance dropped to third the next day, as Belgium's Tom Steels won his second straight stage and moved into second place behind Kirispuu. Lance dropped two more spots, as Italy's Mario Cipollini won the fourth, fifth, sixth, and seventh stages. At this point, Lance also dropped from the headlines. His story was a good one, but unfortunately it looked like a short one. Though still in sixth, just 54 seconds behind, Lance seemed to be fading, just as everyone had expected.

"For me, for the Tour, and for Lance above all, this is the Tour of renewal, of a return to the top level."

JEAN-MARIE LEBLANC,
TOUR DE FRANCE DIRECTOR

MOUNTAIN MAN

chapter 8

"Armstrong's the man of the year. He's come back from so far down, you can't help but admire him."

FRENCH CYCLING STAR LAURENT JALABERT

The entire complexion of the 1999 Tour de France changed on July 11. Worried that saving himself for the mountains would put him too far behind, Lance decided to show the other riders what they were dealing with in that day's 35-mile (56-km) time trial. Displaying awesome power, he covered the distance in 1 hour, 8 minutes, 36 seconds—nearly a minute faster than Zulle, more than 2 minutes ahead of third-place finisher Christophe Moreau, and more than 4 minutes above the other race favorites. It was an incredible performance that catapulted Lance into first place by a whopping 2 minutes, 20 seconds. "It was very long and very difficult," he remembers. "But one of the great victories of my life."

The press went crazy. Believing his comeback was over, reporters had practically written Lance off. Now they were remembering his performance in the mountains in the two June races and wondering if this heroic American might actually be able to extend his lead when the race entered the Alps.

The information collected by Tyler Hamilton during his incredible effort in the Tour de France's eighth-stage time trial enabled Lance to cover the 35 miles (56.5 km) in flawless fashion.

As always, Lance was quick to credit the team. Tyler Hamilton, who started ahead of him, went all out as long as he could, recording his progress every mile so that Lance would know exactly how he was doing at every twist and turn when it was his time to ride. Armed with this information, Lance ended up going so fast that he actually passed several riders who had started minutes ahead of him!

After a well-earned rest day, Lance looked to put more distance between himself and the pack, as the Tour de France entered its first mountain stage. The 132-mile (212-km) course featured five separate climbs. As Lance went up each, he felt even stronger than he had expected. At day's end, he was 31 seconds better than Zulle, who finished

Abraham Olano (right) rode a good race but was unable to chip away at the enormous lead Lance (left) had built up in the early stages.

second. More important, Lance's overall lead, now over Spain's Abraham Olano, grew to 6 minutes, 3 seconds. Not only is that an eternity in a race like the Tour de France, but the fact that it was built in back-to-back stages that included a sprint and mountain climb was extremely intimidating. Instead of wondering what Lance could do, the other riders were beginning to worry that there was nothing Lance *couldn't* do.

They had reason to worry. The next day Lance extended his lead to 7 minutes, 42 seconds. Throughout the Alps, he and his teammates fought fiercely to protect that lead. With a little over a week to go, Lance was looking unbeatable. Several top riders had already dropped out, and several more would follow. Lance, meanwhile, just kept rolling along, maintaining his advantage during the four transitional stages between the Alps and the Pyrenees.

Off the course, things were not so smooth for Lance. With the outcome of the year's most eagerly awaited sporting event all but decided, several European newspapers saw their sales begin to drop off. Sports fans knew that barring a catastrophic crash, Lance was going to win, so many stopped buying the daily paper. In order to stir up controversy and increase sales, several publications began running stories that suggested Lance might be using performance-enhancing drugs. Apparently, the most inspiring comeback story in the history of sports did not provide enough drama for these papers.

Lance was angered by the stories. He had trained too hard and had overcome too much to have these questions raised. "It's disturbing for the sport," he says. "It makes me sick. The bottom line for me is the same as for Miguel Indurain. Sweat is the secret of my success. There's no answer other than hard work."

Lance also pointed out that any reporter who knew anything about cycling should not have been surprised by his performance in the mountains. In preparation for the Tour de France, he had moved to the city of Nice in southern France, so he could train in the very same mountains he was conquering now. "I had never focused on the Tour de France before," he points out. "When I decided to, I was in France the whole time. I lived in France. I raced the whole year in France. My Tour de France preparation was done *in* France!"

The U.S. Postal Service team ignored the controversy and made the most of the Tour's second rest day. Then they prepared to defend Lance's lead through the Pyrenees. The team was getting tired. In the final stages of the race, each rider would have to take his turn leading the pack so that Lance could pedal along in the "slipstream" created by

Superstar Fernando Escartin fails to put any distance between himself and Lance.

*As the riders leave the mountains, Lance's supporters are there to greet him.
American fans poured into France during the race's latter
stages to celebrate Lance's sweet victory.*

his teammates. Concerned for his teammates, Lance took advantage of his big lead and rode more conservatively in this second set of mountains. Meanwhile, one of the sport's best climbers, Fernando Escartin, had some big days in the Pyrenees and moved into a battle for second place. But neither he nor Zulle could close within 6 minutes of Lance.

On the next-to-last day of the race—the third and final time trial—the cycling world prepared to focus on Escartin and Zulle for what promised to be a spirited battle to lock up a second-place finish. Instead, Lance left everyone with one last thrilling performance. With victory just a day away, Lance got an adrenaline rush and put everything he had into the 35-mile (56-km) trial, which was held in gusty winds. Tens of thousands of fans cheered Lance along the way, getting him even more pumped up. As he flashed across the countryside, Lance thought about the fans he had heard were coming from his hometown of Austin to greet him the next day in Paris. He thought about the amazing contributions his teammates had made during the race. And he thought about all the people he had met—some who lost their battle with cancer and some who were still fighting—on his own road to recovery.

Lance completed the course in a dreamlike state. And he finished it 9 seconds better than anyone else. It was simply incredible.

Lance held back nothing during the 19th-stage time trial.
He won it by an incredible 9 seconds.

PARIS AND BEYOND

"I hope what I did in a bike race in France gives hope and inspiration to people around the world."

LANCE ARMSTRONG

More than half a million people were waiting in Paris to greet Lance as he sped down the Champs Elysées toward the finish line on the afternoon of July 25. His final margin of victory over Alex Zulle was 7 minutes, 37 seconds. Lance had performed magnificently and had good luck throughout the race. Only on this final day, when victory was guaranteed, did he run into trouble—a flat tire, of all things! A quick wheel change and Lance was back on the road in no time.

Luck, of course, had little to do with Lance's immense popularity. He was now the king of his sport, as well as its most inspiring

"If you win the Tour de France, the only thing you can do is try to win it again. That's it."

LANCE ARMSTRONG

Karl Haussmann checks Lance's progress online. Haussmann is the director of the Lance Armstrong Foundation.

story. He had won the Tour de France with flair, using a style that blended aggressive attacks with quick thinking and cool calculation. And the fans adored it. "I've always said that I'd rather be the guy that lights up the race and finishes second, than the guy that sits back, doesn't do anything, and wins," he says.

Lance became only the second American to win the Tour de France and the first to win it as a member of an American team. That meant a lot to him. He was tired of hearing that U.S. teams were second-rate. In his mind, his teammates were tougher than anyone, and they proved it in this race. Even though the Postal Service team had never had to protect a leader in a race like this, everyone knew his job and did his job. "When we got the jersey [in the eighth stage] and said we would defend it, people thought we were crazy," he recalls. "They said this team isn't strong enough. Well, they proved they're the strongest team in the race."

After his amazing victory, Lance flew back to the United States on Nike's private jet for a crazy 24 hours. He posed for several magazine photo shoots, did a few TV interviews, visited the New York Stock Exchange, shot a video,

Did You Know?

Thanks to Lance's hard work, both on and off the bike, The Lance Armstrong Foundation is a leader in the fight against cancer. The foundation's efforts are aimed at awareness, education, and research.

What's the big deal? After his Tour de France win, Lance flew to New York to do magazine and television interviews and appear on THE LATE SHOW WITH DAVID LETTERMAN.

negotiated a movie deal, and appeared on *The Late Show with David Letterman*. He then recrossed the Atlantic to appear in a series of five European exhibition races. Lance and Kristin also threw a huge party at their house in Nice, France.

When Lance returned to his hometown in August, the city of Austin threw him a Texas-style parade and party with tons of food and five bands. An estimated 4,000 cyclists rode in front of Lance and Kristin, who waved to the crowd from the backseat of a white convertible. Thousands more lined Congress Avenue, many wearing yellow jerseys to commemorate his victory. Yellow balloons were everywhere. Mayor Kirk Watson and Governor George Bush were on hand, and Lance presented Bush with one of the yellow jerseys he earned during the race. "There were times when it seemed to all be falling away," Lance told a cheering crowd. "There were people who stood by me in this city. They became my family. We're here to celebrate two things—not just victory in the Tour de France but victory over a dreadful illness. It has to be a celebration of survival."

The next day Lance, his mom, and Kristin arrived in Washington, D.C., where Lance addressed the National Press Club. From there, the Armstrongs went to the White House, where they met President Bill Clinton in the Oval Office. Next, he made an appearance with a group of young cancer survivors and Vice President Al Gore, who planned to make fighting cancer a key theme in his 2000 presidential campaign. That evening, they attended a reception for the U.S. Postal Service team.

The next day found the Armstrongs back in Austin, where Lance visited doctors for a checkup. They drew blood, X-rayed his chest, and gave him a clean bill of health. There is always the chance the cancer will come back, but it is now just a slim chance— no more than 2 or 3 percent.

In late August, Lance proved he is a man of his word. He competed in a mountain bike rally and finished sixth in a cross-country race. Two days later he entered the short-track event, riding 16 laps around a quarter-mile course. Lance had never competed in this type of event. After a few laps he found his brakes clogged with mud and his goggles so fogged up he peeled them off and threw them away. Then he pedaled his heart out and finished fourth. No one in the crowd could quite believe this mud-covered maniac was the same guy who had just won the biggest race in the world. Why was he even here? "It was fun," Lance insists.

President Clinton checks out a couple of gifts from Lance during a ceremony in the White House rose garden.

CYCLE SPORT

ARMSTRONG
THE TEXAN TORNADO SWEEPS
TO HIS FIRST TOUR WIN

TOUR DE FRANCE
100-PAGE REVIEW

CREDIT LYONNAIS

September 1999 $6.25

MERCKX'S 1969 TOUR WIN REMEMBERED LEMOND ON ARMSTRONG

*It was hard to find a cycling magazine that did not have
Lance on its cover following his Tour de France victory.*

Kristen Armstrong watches as her husband signs autographs for traders on the floor of the New York Stock Exchange during his visit to New York. Kristin and Lance were married in May 1999.

What Lance does not say is that he agreed to enter this rally many months before he won the Tour de France. He could have called promoters and demanded more money to show up. Or he could have said he wasn't feeling well and skipped it altogether. He decided instead to live up to his promise. "Money isn't that important," he explains. "The illness changed a lot of that. Before, I was motivated by making money. Now I'd rather have my health than money."

According to Lance, there are only two drawbacks to winning the Tour de France. First, he and Kristin found it hard to have any quiet time together. Everyone wanted a piece of Lance, and even Kristin ended up doing interviews with magazines and television shows. Normally, the happy couple would have been content to ride it out and take their private time after all the commotion died down. But for Kristin and Lance, the commotion was just about to begin. In October their first child, Luke, was born.

The second drawback? Lance found it hard to stick to his diet. All the parties, parades, personal appearances, and talk shows made it difficult to eat smart. "For nine months, I ate like a *monk*," he laughs. "Since the night the race ended, I've been eating what I like—fries, beer, ice cream, hamburgers. Life has been extremely hectic."

Lance is the winner of the Tour de France. No one can ever take that away from him. But that is *what* he is, not *who* he is. Lance is the first to tell you, he's a *cancer survivor* first, last, and always. "I'm proud to be a cancer survivor," he says. "This race and my performance are going to affect a lot of people in a positive, wonderful, fantastic way."

Lance believes that what he has accomplished will bring hope to others, and that his very public triumph over cancer will convince people not to make the same mistake he did and wait until the disease has spread before seeking help. He also hopes his Lance Armstrong Foundation can save lives and raise awareness.

Did You Know?

After Lance's victory, cycling shops instantly sold out of red-white-and-blue zip-front U.S. Postal team jerseys. The manufacturer, Pearl Izumi, had to go into high gear to meet the incredible demand. They sold more than 10,000!

Lance has also come to terms with his cancer on a different level. He actually credits his illness with making him a better athlete, and a better person. "I have come to learn and grow, and now I know that's the best thing that ever happened to me," he says. "The opportunities I have encountered have been immensely great.

"I'm enjoying this," Lance says of his sudden celebrity. "It won't last forever. You lose the fame and the recognition, it all goes away. I know that. I'm not addicted to this. I have to know that in 10 years' time I'll be another 'ex-athlete.' And that's fine with me. Maybe some people will remember me, but people forget. The cause—the foundation—will live on."

So will Lance's remarkable story. His comeback will forever give those stricken with cancer inspiration to keep fighting and never give up. For everyone else, Lance Armstrong will stand as a monument to the triumph of the human spirit in the face of desperate odds.

If anyone knows how to enjoy the fame and fortune that comes with winning your sport's most famous event, it is Lance. No athlete has ever come so far back after being so far down. Sometimes, Lance himself can hardly believe it.

INDEX
page numbers in *italics* refer to illustrations